LIVING THE
Eternal Promise

A guide for individual
or group reflection and action

by **Colin Saxton**

Friends United Press

Friends United Press
101 Quaker Hill Drive
Richmond, IN 47374
friendspress@fum.org
shop.fum.org

ISBN 978-0-944350-76-8

Preface

In preparation for the 2017 Friends United Meeting Triennial in Wichita, Kansas, Friends United Press is republishing Thomas Kelly's *The Eternal Promise* in both hardcopy and digitized editions. This 2017 Triennial is gathering under the banner of *A Living Flame*, a phrase lifted from this particular work by Friend Kelly.

Around the Quaker world, there is a murmuring restlessness and growing hunger for a deeper and more vibrant spiritual experience. Especially in the context of our North American churches and meetings, Friends frequently express the desire to know and be known by that which is truly Eternal; to establish authentic faith communities kindled and animated by the Power and Presence of the Holy Spirit; and to move beyond endless human striving in order to fully partner in the Way of the Living Christ—all to the glory of God and for the sake of the world.

The Eternal Promise is one invitation into this way of life. To encourage its reading and to facilitate reflection and conversation across the Friends' world, Friends United Press created this companion volume—*Living the Eternal Promise: A Study Guide*. We encourage you to use it as a starter kit for personal reflection and a launch pad for group discussion. Rather than being limited by the queries and suggestions for reflection and action, we urge you to modify any and all of it as is helpful. Expand on what is written here. Improve upon these offering in ways that take you deeper into the heart of Christ, enable you to engage one another more fully, and ready you for faithful service.

Introduction

In 1981, after a few years of dark depression, drug abuse, and rapidly growing despair over the state of the world, I met Jesus. It was an encounter that upended me, turning most of my world inside out and upside down. Now thirty-five years later, I still feel the blessed reverberations of this first meeting.

It began with a simple prayer, "I have no idea what it means—but I will follow you." I was not so much seeking respite and refuge from my demons, as much as I was startled and awestruck by the depth of God's goodness and mercy for me and all of creation. In my encounter with the Living Christ, I found what I did not know I was even searching for—a God who can be known, who actively loves all of humanity, and who is deeply engaged in restoring a broken world.

Words fail to describe the shift that took place in me at that time. Tearstains on the pages of this study guide might better represent the joy, freedom, and peace I came to know in those early days. An overwhelming sense of Mercy washed over me with such force, I could hardly bear it at times. My eyes kept being opened to a Glory more vivid and real than I ever imagined possible. Unshackled from my earlier despair, I found myself becoming what the prophet Zechariah describes—a prisoner of Hope. Indeed, I was so captured and captivated by God's vision for the world, I longed to serve in any and every way possible. I believed then, as I do now, that God's will is meant to be lived out on earth just as it is in heaven.

Eventually, of course, "reality" set in. My own immaturity, ignorance, self-centeredness, and human limitations butted-up against the ideal of perpetual faithfulness and ongoing intimacy with God. The journey from sinner to saint, I quickly learned, was going to be painstaking and humbling. In my case, it was surely going to last a lifetime—probably much longer!

Thankfully, I found my way into a small group of more experienced, kindred souls. It was this community that began to train and sustain me. Prayer was a foreign language. Bible study was a whole new experience. Learning to walk in the Way of Christ meant traveling in unfamiliar territory. I learned much from these companions, and their expert help and guidance was just what I needed to not give up or wander too far off course.

During part of our time together, the group worked through Richard Foster's *Celebration of Discipline*, a helpful primer for contemplative spirituality. At this time, I knew next to nothing about Quakers and had never, to my knowledge, met one. But over the course of the book, my interest in Friends was piqued. I had just begun a deliberate search for a larger faith community to plant roots in and call home. Before long, the Friends in Northwest Yearly Meeting became my family. They were the mother that raised and nurtured me with tender, loving care.

In addition to introducing me to Quakers, *Celebration of Discipline* also introduced me to Thomas Kelly. Scattered references throughout the book point to him and I was drawn to the way Foster described Kelly's impact and his vision of spirituality. Before too long, I devoured *Testament of Devotion* several times and eventually found *The Eternal Promise*. Both books hold a special place in my library. I imagine I have read both books well over a dozen times each.

I keep returning to Kelly, in part, because I always rediscover a rare and precious commodity that is less apparent in other spiritual authors. Sadly, it is even less common in conversations I have with others about God. This rare quality is greater than optimism and more profound than idealism. Instead, I describe it as a sense of "holy expectancy." At least for me, I need regular and persistent reminders that a life of holy expectancy is more than possible—it is available and waiting to be embraced. As I read and re-read *The Eternal Promise*, I find myself confronted about how passionately I am truly pursuing God and comforted by how passionately God is pursuing me. Just as I begin to question the possibility of encountering Christ on the deepest level, Kelly reminds me that He is as close as my very breath—waiting to be rediscovered once more. Kelly says, in essence:

Live in Holy Expectancy!

Do you hunger and thirst to know Christ and the intimate love of God? Turn to Him now!

Do you long to have the Life and Power of God coursing through you? Yield to it this very moment!

Do you wish to be used for God's glory and the good others each and every moment of your life? Wonderful—for this is God's deepest longing, as well!

Do you hunger and thirst for a fellowship of kindred, kindled souls who are setting the world aflame with God's Light? Beautiful! You are already knit together and ready to be used! Become the Children of Light!

What I love best about this vision of expectancy is Kelly's unblinking realism. He knows and communicates the costliness of this way. We don't seek the Kingdom of God by making minor adjustments to our regularly scheduled program or undergoing a few inconveniences to make God happy. We don't alter our plans and personal agendas—they must be abandoned. The doorway to the Eternal Promise is found in daily dying to oneself and in the passionate, joyful pursuit of God, and God alone. Am I willing to walk through that door? This is the costly decision we each get to make as individuals and one our community gets to face together—if we are willing.

Having just finished reading *The Eternal Promise* again, I am mindful how far I still have to go in my journey and how deeply grateful I am for grace in getting there. Even so, I continue to live in holy expectancy. I expect a life of deep communion with the Living Christ. I expect to be part of a beloved fellowship of Friends, united in love and joined in a common purpose. I expect to participate in God's restoration of the cosmos, living into the calling and invitation to be the hands and feet of Christ. I expect others feel exactly the same. What about you?

Suggestions for Engaging and Exploring *The Eternal Promise*

There is no one *right* way to read a book. Some of us are skimmers, hop-skip-and-jumping our way across the ideas and images that most capture our attention. Others of us linger over each and every word, puzzling over possible meanings and searching for deeper connections that may or may not have been intended by the author. Some of us feel most comfortable in the pristine pages of an unmarked text. Others highlight in multi-colors or scrawl chicken-scratch notes into the margins that become impossible to decipher later. Some revel in exploring a book with companions who may offer alternate impressions or even sharp differences of opinion. For some, quiet solitude is just the right environs to befriend a new book.

In whatever way you best read and reflect, my hope is you will find a path to get beneath the black-on-white words tattooed on each page of *The Eternal Promise*. In fact, my prayer is that each of us will not so much read the text *as be read by it*. At its best, sacred writing is not about acquiring information to store away for another day. It is about uncovering: truths about God, about ourselves, and about the world we inhabit. Such uncovering is a grace, exposing us to a light and love that may just kindle something new within us or lift us to a higher plain. Even when the light is uncomfortable and creates a shadow—exposing something broken, wounded, and buried within us—it may become a grace that mends, heals and frees us in the future.

In each chapter, there are three sets of queries and suggestions. The first set is for **personal reflection.** Even if you choose to be part of a small group, you may wish to reflect on these as you read through the text by yourself. You will notice there is room in each batch of queries to formulate one or more of your own. Please take this suggestion seriously. Maybe there is a query or suggestion God is seeking to explore *with you*—one speaking directly to your condition. If so, be encouraged to give your best time and attention to it!

The next set of queries and suggestions is created for a **group conversation.** Maybe your Meeting or Church is using this study guide during Sunday School or First Day School or in a small group. If Friends are willing, it may serve you best to have each person read the chapter in advance of meeting. Some selections are longer than others and some sets of queries might take time—and tenderness—to wade into and work through together. Give yourself time and space for these holy conversations. If it is helpful and an option in the schedule, some chapters and responses might be better spread over multiple weeks.

Finally, there is a list of suggestions for **living into the Eternal Promise.** It is not necessarily intended that all of these be adopted. Some will take planning. Others may fit better in another season of life. If you find some silly or inappropriate for your situation—ignore them. Again, the option always exists to consider, plan and implement your own ideas.

In each case, explore the text with an open heart. What is God saying to me? To us? What is being asked of me? Am I willing?

As Friends from all around the world share in the exploration of Thomas Kelly's wonderful little book, who knows how God just might use it to shake us from our slumber and refashion us into the Children of Light. Blessings as you explore *The Eternal Promise* and find yourselves being explored by God's Presence!

1

SECTION ONE

Religion for this Distraught World

By the time Thomas Kelly finished the last of the four essays in this chapter, in 1940, the world was once again plunging into a catastrophic season of warfare. The great spirit of hopefulness in human ingenuity and social progress—so common in the early twentieth century—was now being vanquished by another painful lesson in our equal capacity for evil and social destruction. For many, "distraught" was a word that best captured the sense of profound despair and agitation over the present and for the future.

A similar mood hovers over us in our day. Despite amazing advances in medicine, technology, social justice and even peacemaking, too many people are wrapped up in fear and distress. The intensity of our political and ideological differences make us suspicious of one another. Civility and engagement are giving way to polemic debates and cultural isolationism. Sociologists measure our growing feelings of hopelessness and loneliness.

In many parts of the world, Christianity is growing and thriving. In the United States and Europe, however, interest and participation in organized religion is declining. Maybe "distraught" still captures the mood of our day. What alternative are we called to embody and offer to others?

WEEK ONE
American Christianity

QUERIES AND SUGGESTIONS FOR PERSONAL REFLECTION

1. Do I have a genuine and passionate hunger to know God? If not, what hinders this? What do I most need at this point in my life to stimulate and satisfy this hunger?

2. Where is my experience of God leading me into the world? Are there particular issues or concerns to which I am feeling called, and which I feel empowered to engage? What is the next right step I am led to take in this journey?

3. Am I more inclined to be a person gazing into heaven, or hustling to go and change the world? How am I being called to a greater sense of equilibrium around my inward devotion and outward service?

4. What other queries am I being led to consider?

QUERIES AND SUGGESTIONS FOR GROUP CONVERSATION

1. Within American churches generally and Quaker gatherings specifically, we are often encouraged to "change the world." What are the strengths and weaknesses of this message? Are we, in fact, called to change the world? If so, how?

2. Kelly says *"The straightest road to social gospel runs through profound mystical experience."* Is this true in our lives? What does he mean by mystical experience, and how do we practice this in our fellowship?

3. In what ways is the Divine Life being channeled through us into our community or around the world? Are there ways this Life is being hindered from flowing through us? If so, how and what might we do about it?

4. What other queries are we being led to consider?

LIVING INTO THE ETERNAL PROMISE

1. Each day this week, spend five minutes (or more!) alone with God. Pray, **"Christ, let me know you and your love for the world."** What do you see, hear, or sense as you pray this?

2. Throughout the week, pay attention to all of the messages calling you to take action—from social media, television, neighbors, Church/Meeting, etc. List all of them and what you are being asked to do. How do you feel about this list? Among the items listed, are there particular ones which stir your soul?

3. What other steps am I being called to take?

WEEK TWO
Christians and Decided Christians

QUERIES AND SUGGESTIONS FOR PERSONAL REFLECTION

1. Kelly describes a "decided Christian" with words like "joyful," "glad readiness," "integration," and "peace." How well do these words describe my life as a follower of Christ? What does my answer reflect about the condition of my soul?

2. What would the end of "tolerated double-mindedness" mean for me? Are there changes I need to make in how I am living? Is there some new direction I need to take in order to be more singularly devoted to God?

3. Kelly implies that the decided life is best lived in community. Who are the people who encourage my deepest faithfulness and most passionate pursuit of God? Have I communicated to them how I depend on them in this way? Are there people who are depending on me in this manner? Am I being faithful in supporting and encouraging them in the ways they most need?

4. What other queries am I being led to consider?

QUERIES AND SUGGESTIONS FOR GROUP CONVERSATION

1. Are there ways in which we are settling for a "mere Christianity" rather than embracing a "decided Christianity" within our community? How so?

2. When others look at and experience our fellowship, do they find an *authentic and vital* Christianity? Have

we ever asked any neighbors, visitors, or trustworthy friends how they view our Meeting/Church? If so, what did they say? If not—how might we go about doing this?

3. How might we begin to discern and intentionally create an authentic and vital fellowship in our place and time? What would a "homeland for the soul" look like for us?

4. What other queries are we being led to consider?

LIVING INTO THE ETERNAL PROMISE

1. Kelly suggests that there are many people around us who are sincere, honest, and even desperate in their search for God. Who do you know like this? Commit to pray for this person throughout the week—and if you are willing, to be given an opportunity to speak with this person about faith and life in Christ.

2. In his book *Encounter with Silence*, John Punshon writes:*"I understand Jesus to be saying that if I truly desire to follow him and to enter the kingdom of heaven, I must be willing to open my heart completely, give everything I have and hold nothing back in my own secret places. I must, in a word, be willing to be searched myself. I must bring all those things that make me the person I am, good and bad, acceptable and unacceptable, and place them before God. I must, to use a special Quaker phrase, "come to the light."* During the course of this week, take half an hour for solitude. In the Presence of Christ, open yourself in the way Punshon describes. What do you hear? How will you respond?

3. What other steps am I being called to take?

WEEK THREE

Excerpts from
the Richard Cary Lecture

QUERIES AND SUGGESTIONS FOR PERSONAL REFLECTION

1. Kelly contrasts a life where I remain at the center and one in which God is the Center. Several avenues for "de-selfing" emerge in this chapter—releasing control, worship, entering into the sufferings of others, not taking ourselves so seriously, etc. What are the spiritual disciplines and practices that best help me become centered in Christ and less self-centered?

2. After reading this chapter, consider these phrases:

   We are meant to be witnesses of that which we have seen and our hands have handled of the word of Life. (p.6)

   Surrender of self to that indwelling Life is entrance upon an astounding, an almost miraculous Life. (p.7)

   Calm replaces strain, peace replaces anxiety. (p.7)

   Life itself becomes a sacrament wherein sin is blasphemy. (p.7)

   A deep longing for personal righteousness and purity sets in. (p.7)

   Paul speaks truly when he says that we are no longer live, but Christ lives in us, dynamic, energetic, creative, persuasive. (p.8)

God is no longer the object of belief; He is a Reality, who has continued, within us, His real Presence in the world. (p.9)

3. Which of these are true in my experience?

4. Which of these ring less true?

5. For Kelly, the experience of God's love naturally moves us toward a deeper love for all others. Who are the ones I am feeling most challenged to love right now? Am I willing to pray for the grace to love even these?

6. What other queries am I being led to consider?

QUERIES AND SUGGESTIONS FOR GROUP CONVERSATION

1. Around the circle, share a few of the vivid and life-altering encounters when we have been found by God and have, indeed, witnessed the Resurrected Christ at work in our lives and in the world.

2. In a spirit of prayer and worship, read the fourth paragraph beginning "How different is the experience of Life…"

3. As one individual reads the text, each one listen for a particular word or phrase that catches your attention. Go around the circle sharing the word or phrase. Allow a few moments of silence between sharing.

4. Have another person read the paragraph once more. Going around the circle, briefly reflect on why or how that word or phrase is meaningful to each of us. Once again, take a few moments for silence between sharing.

5. Finally, read it one more time. As you take turns sharing around the circle, have each member of the group reflect on what action(s) the text may be prompting any to take.

6. What other queries are we being led to consider?

LIVING INTO THE ETERNAL PROMISE

1. Kelly invites us to "unclasp the clenched fists of self-resolution, to be pliant in His firm guidance, sensitive to the inflections of the inner voice." In a time of prayer this week, consider the things you are gripping too tightly and having a hard time releasing to God's care. Do you trust your ability to manage these better than God? Name each one and imagine holding them, one by one, in your open hand. Now clench your fist and hold it as tightly as you possibly can for as long as you can. In prayer, and as an act of surrender, release your grip on the things you are honestly willing to let go of—to give over to the care and control of God.

2. Consider the callouses that have grown tough and thick around your heart. Are there particular people, problems or painful situations that have left you hardened and self-protective? Have you grown indifferent, apathetic, or insensitive to someone or something God is calling you to love and engage? Confess this to God and pray for a tendered, open spirit. If needed, pray for a willingness *to be willing* to re-enter this situation or relationship. If you have a close friend whom you trust, confess this need in your life to them and ask them to pray for your growing tenderness and openness. Do not rush to re-engage this

matter—move only as you actually feel enabled and led to do so with grace and clarity.

3. As you prepare to come to worship on Sunday/First Day, pray that Christ might be fully present in the Meeting and at work gathering the fellowship. As you settle into worship, focus on being a channel for the Holy Spirit to work. Look around the room and pray for each and every member of the Body. Allow the love of God to flow through you, as you bless and hold each member in the Presence of Christ.

4. What other steps am I being called to take?

WEEK FOUR
Religion for this Distraught World

QUERIES AND SUGGESTIONS FOR PERSONAL REFLECTION

1. Kelly writes of the "totalitarian claims of the gospel." What does this mean in your understanding and experience? Examine the attitudes and actions that may not yet be in harmony with this vision of life.

2. How do I appropriately discern how to be "ready for new truth" and yet hold on to "the old that is true and must be kept?"

3. Thomas Kelly says that "perpetual open-mindedness" becomes a detriment to faith, stands in the way of commitment and purpose. "There is a need for positive drive and conviction," he says. How do I respond to this? Is this relevant to my life?

4. What other queries am I being led to consider?

QUERIES AND SUGGESTIONS FOR GROUP CONVERSATION

1. How do we avoid unnecessary uniformity but still encourage an essential unity when it comes to living out our faith?

2. Would our Church/Meeting benefit by developing a clear and mutually-shared sense of identity and common mission? If so, how might we intentionally move in this direction?

3. Kelly suggests a need for a "third order"—a quasi-monastic movement aimed at intentionally living into the Way of Jesus through our ordinary lives. What barriers do we encounter in our quest for this life? How might we better support one another in pursuing this third way?

4. What other queries are we being led to consider?

LIVING INTO THE ETERNAL PROMISE

1. Commit to reading through the four Gospels and book of Acts over the next several months. Read at least one chapter a day if possible. Journal on those passages which refer to the Kingdom of God. What is God teaching you through your reading?

2. If you have not done so, consider writing a personal mission statement. Many free online resources provide useful suggestions for how to do this and offer examples to consider.

   - Take adequate time to formalize a statement that clearly and succinctly articulates your sense of God-given purpose. Make sure it describes the essential values you seek to uphold and forms a foundation for setting goals. Be sure it captures who you are and intend to be in a way that inspires you to action.
   - Connect with a few trusted friends and ask them to help you evaluate your life-direction in view of this mission statement. Ask them to meet with you over the course of several weeks for prayer and discernment around questions like these:

- In what ways am currently living into this sense of mission?
- Are there areas in my life misaligned with this statement?
- What new directions am I being led to consider?
- What additional support, training, accountability, encouragement do I need to live most faithfully?

3. What other steps am I being called to take?

WEEK FIVE
Where are the Signs of Hope?

QUERIES AND SUGGESTIONS FOR PERSONAL REFLECTION

1. What have been the lowest, most desperate times in my journey? As I look back on those moments now, what were the signs or source of hope that eventually appeared?

2. Who are the people in my life who may be feeling hopeless? What authentic message of hope do I have to offer others?

3. Kelly describes the Seed of Christ as "amazing and dangerous." In what ways am I experiencing the amazing aspects of Christ within? In what ways is this Presence feeling dangerous to me, and why?

4. What other queries am I being led to consider?

QUERIES AND SUGGESTIONS FOR GROUP CONVERSATION

1. In what ways does our Meeting/Church genuinely enter into the sufferings of others?

2. How do we serve as a visible witness to hope? How do we communicate this hope in our words and message to others?

3. Quakers are sometimes reticent to verbally share our faith with others. Why is this so? What are appropriate, winsome, and invitational ways to share our

faith? Who are the people in our community who seem to have a gift for sharing the Good News and how can we encourage their ministry?

4. What other queries are we being led to consider?

LIVING INTO THE ETERNAL PROMISE

1. In prayer this week, focus on renouncing these things:

    - My perceived "right" to life, liberty, and the pursuit of happiness.
    - My well-intentioned but misplaced efforts to "save the world."
    - My desire for fame, recognition, acclamation.
    - My tendency toward pride, self-importance, and control over others and my circumstances.

2. In addition to renunciation, build into your time of prayer a receptivity to these gifts and graces:

    - A life-transforming knowledge of God's unconditional love and forgiveness, freedom to be who God has created me to be, and the ability to be faithful in each and every circumstance.
    - A willingness be used for others' good and God's glory in the midst of my ordinary life.
    - A renewed spirit of humility, service, and surrender to God's good will.

3. Identify one courageous and hopeful action you can take each day that demonstrates the Light of Christ is overcoming the world's darkness.

4. What other steps am I being called to take?

2

SECTION TWO
The Publishers of Truth

As a spiritual community, Friends have their own distinct story and relatively unique characteristics. Within the larger Christian movement, there are wonderful ways in which Quakers stand out.

In the North American context, a consistent narrative describes most people as being deeply "spiritual" but not "religious." What this actually means and how it impacts faith communities is not always easy to pinpoint. Reporters frequently state, however, that many people are searching for an experiential faith, one that offers meaning and purpose, a faith that is engaged in real-world issues, one offering an authentic sense of community and opportunity for all to participate and lead. More interestingly, people also name values like peacemaking, justice, equality, and simplicity as necessary aspects of any spiritual path they would choose.

In many ways, these times appear to be ready-made for Quakers to engage our cultures in a transformational way, to offer an invitation to life with God and a home within a beloved fellowship of Friends. And yet many of our Churches, Meetings and regional gathering are in decline and embroiled in conflict. In the face of this opportunity, what alternative are we called to embody and offer to others?

WEEK SIX
The Quaker Discovery

QUERIES AND SUGGESTIONS FOR PERSONAL REFLECTION

Kelly asks several searching queries of his own in this chapter. Reflect on them:

1. Am I down in the flaming center of God?

2. Have I come into the deeps, where the soul meets God and knows His love and power?

3. Have I discovered God as a living Immediacy, a sweet Presence and stirring, life-renovating power within me?

4. Do I walk by his guidance, feeding every day, like knights of the Grail, on the body and blood of Christ, knowing every day and every act to be a sacrament?

5. What other queries am I being led to consider?

QUERIES AND SUGGESTIONS FOR GROUP CONVERSATION

1. Thomas Kelly offers a sobering and discouraging depiction of the state of Friends in his day. After reading the second paragraph (on page 28) aloud in your gathering, reflect on these queries:

   • In what ways does this description reflect the condition of Friends in our time?

- If we had to describe our Meeting or Church in ten words or less, what would we say? (It might be useful to have each member take a few moments to consider this and write down their response before sharing it).
- Are we happy or content with these descriptions? If not, what do we do about it?

2. It has been said that "Quakerism is always a first-generation faith." That is, it must be experienced afresh by each individual and every new generation if it is to remain vital.

- If this is true, how do we intentionally encourage newcomers to find a deep and life-transforming relationship with the Living God rather than settling for something less?
- Again, assuming this is true, how do we help our children and grandchildren to appropriate their own vibrant faith, rather than unintentionally settling into the "respectable, complacent and comfortable" confines of a birth-right religion?

3. What other queries are we being led to consider?

LIVING INTO THE ETERNAL PROMISE

1. Begin each day this week (and beyond, if helpful) by reading this modified version of Romans 12:1-2. Use it as a reminder that true worship and faithfulness begin by opening ourselves to Christ's Presence and Power:

I plead with you, beloved, in view of God's overwhelming mercy, take your ordinary life—the one you live every day—and give it as a gift to God, all you do and say. This is the highest act of worship. Do not conform and adjust to the pressure of the world around you, making you immature and misshapen. Instead, be transformed by fixing your attention on God. Then you will know and follow God's good, pleasing and perfect will.

2. Throughout the day, *practice* being attentive to Christ. Consider some simple ways to remember you live and walk in the Light of Christ each and every moment. These include:

- Skip one meal each day this week and devote the time to listening and prayer.
- Set your alarm to go off each hour as a reminder to give thanks and pray throughout the day.
- Focus your attention on praying for each person you encounter this week. Ask God to flood them with mercy and love in every circumstance. Imagine the Light of Christ surrounding each one.
- Eliminate as many unnecessary distractions as possible. This week, take a sabbatical from as much technology and other over-stimulation as you can, in order to attend to the Inward Teacher and Guide.
- Ask your closest friends to hold you in prayer this week—helping you be especially attentive to God's presence and responsive to God's leading.

3. As your last act of devotion for the day, spend fifteen minutes in prayer in this way:

- Ask God for light. Pray for the ability to see the day through God's eyes, not merely your own. Where/when did you most sense Christ's presence? When did you feel most distant? Is there anything to learn from these observations?
- Give thanks. The day just lived is a gift from God. Be grateful for it.
- Review the day. Carefully look back on the day just completed, being guided by the Holy Spirit. Is there anything I have been taught that I need to remember or act upon?
- Face your shortcomings. Have I harmed others or broken fellowship with anyone? Is there some wrong I need to now confess to God? Do I need to be reconciled with anyone?
- Look toward the day to come. Where do I most need God to meet me tomorrow?

4. What other steps am I being called to take?

WEEK SEVEN
Quakers and Symbolism

QUERIES AND SUGGESTIONS FOR PERSONAL REFLECTION

1. What aspects of this chapter most spoke to my condition?

2. Are there ways in which I sometimes settle for symbols rather than pushing deeper toward the Reality beyond the symbol?

3. The ability to communicate my experience of Christ is both vitally important and always imperfect, since words cannot adequately describe the mystery and immensity of God. But what *can I say?* If pressed to explain my experience of Christ—what would I say?

4. What other queries am I being led to consider?

QUERIES AND SUGGESTIONS FOR GROUP CONVERSATION

1. Kelly reminds us that "the danger in symbols which Quakers fear is that *life* will go out of the symbol, leaving it an empty shell, a static form, cruelly confining or killing out the living movement of the spirit."

   - How has this been true (or not) in our experience?
   - Is it possible that the *absence of symbols* can have the same effect? If so, how?

2. It is often mistakenly stated, "Quakers don't practice baptism or communion." Though most do not rely on the actual water, wine, or bread for either ritual or

ceremonial use, we *do intend* to live out our baptism and into our communion with God and one another. How do we practically go about this? Are there ways we might deepen these essential experiences on a communal level?

3. A significant social issue in Kelly's day revolved around race relations. Given the ongoing racial, tribal, and class tensions in many parts of the world, what creative lived behaviors—rather than symbolic gestures—might we engage in to foster equality?

4. What other queries are we being led to consider?

LIVING INTO THE ETERNAL PROMISE

1. Understanding the origins and history of our movement is a way to help us live more fully into the present and future. Reflect on the areas of our Friends faith in which you would like to learn more. Visit your Meeting/Church's library. Talk to the pastor or clerk of your Meeting about books that might be of help. Go to the FUM website (fum.org) to find out more about Quakers or visit the Friends United Press site (shop.fum.org) to find other physical or virtual resources.

2. Authentically living into the Divine Life, according to Kelly, includes a willingness to drop undertakings as much as it means to start undertakings when led of the Spirit. As part of your ongoing journey, spend some time this week asking God if there are any specific commitments, responsibilities, roles you are being released from or are now asked to drop.

3. What other steps am I being called to take?

WEEK EIGHT
The Gathered Meeting

QUERIES AND SUGGESTIONS FOR PERSONAL REFLECTION

1. How do I make myself ready for gathered worship? What practices throughout the week prepare me to be a kindled presence on Sunday morning? Do I faithfully prepare in this way?

2. Am I willing to speak in worship if led? How do I know if Christ is calling on me to share a message with the gathered community or not?

3. What expectations do I bring to worship? Are these helpful to me and to others?

4. What other queries am I being led to consider?

QUERIES AND SUGGESTIONS FOR GROUP CONVERSATION

1. In our experience of gathered worship, what have been the most transforming moments? When has Christ's Presence been most vivid to us?

2. Within our community of faith—whether our style of worship is programmed or unprogrammed—how do we intentionally make space for God to be the director and leader of our worship?

3. Are there ways our community is unintentionally blocking the freedom and movement of the Spirit in our midst? How might we lovingly address these barriers?

4. What other queries are we being led to consider?

LIVING INTO THE ETERNAL PROMISE

1. Establish a pattern and practice of coming to worship prepared. Pray for the community and the time together in advance of the Meeting. Surrender your own will and expectations prior to arriving. As you take your place in the Meetinghouse, look around the room and into the faces of each person present. In that moment, remember that "you are written on one another's hearts," and pray for this Body to experience the fullness of being united in Christ this day.

2. If you know you are at odds with someone in the Church/Meeting—go and seek to resolve the matter prior to Sunday. Practice the command of Jesus (Matthew 5:23-24) to be reconciled to one another before coming to worship God.

3. On a morning when you have trouble centering or find it difficult to focus on God, turn your attention to someone else in the fellowship. Spend the time simply praying for that person. Become a channel for God's love and grace to be poured out upon them. Imagine God's love flowing through your hands and directly into their heart. Don't be surprised if they notice.

4. What other steps am I being called to take?

WEEK NINE
The Publishers of Truth

1. When it comes to faithfully following Christ, am I more inclined to *fear excess* or *fear caution?* In either case, what is the source of that fear and how might I overcome it?

2. The author describes a person being so blinded by God's splendor that they will not give in to the inevitable discouragement or disillusionment that comes from being part of a Meeting or Church. Is this me? Do I believe this is possible? Why?

3. If given one minute to give a message to the members of my Meeting/Church—what would I say to them?

4. What other queries am I being led to consider?

QUERIES AND SUGGESTIONS FOR GROUP CONVERSATION

1. Kelly holds out hope for a church rekindled and serving as an amazing and powerful agent of transformation in the world. What would this look like in our community? In what ways are we moving in that direction?

2. How are we fostering a sense of fellowship that shares in "a common understanding, a common mission, a common Life and Love . . . and . . . an opportunity to know one another in that which is eternal?"

3. As a Meeting/Church, do we unintentionally do anything that dampens or quenches the spiritual passion or unreserved faithfulness of others ?

4. What other queries are we being led to consider?

LIVING INTO THE ETERNAL PROMISE

1. Decide again—in this moment—to dedicate your whole self, without reservation to the person of Christ and the passionate pursuit of God's Kingdom.

2. Consider and name the ways in which you remain cautious and reserved in your life of faith and service. What is controlling your actions in these areas?

3. If you do not yet have an intimate circle of Friends, in which you are finding deep fellowship, spiritual accountability and support, begin praying earnestly to receive this gift. Who comes to mind? Initiate a conversation with others to see if each might be similarly searching for this kind of community.

4. What other steps am I being called to take?

3

SECTION THREE
Room for the Infinite

On World Quaker Day a few years ago, I was asked to speak on the theme, "What in the World are Quakers Doing?" It was hoped I might highlight some of the Friends projects and programs being carried out by the many Quaker organizations working around the globe.

I began the message by saying, "What are Quakers *not* doing?!? As far as I can see we are involved in just about everything!" Actually, the quality and quantity of activity is impressive for such a small band of people—justice, reconciliation, lobbying, church planting, medicine, education, evangelism, relief, leadership training—the list goes on and on.

There are days, however, when our endless striving and tireless work catches up with us. If we are not careful, it can breed cynicism, despair, pride, and arrogance. We can fall into the trap of running ahead of our Guide or becoming so exhausted we give up along the way. In a world that often struggles to perceive the Presence or note the activity of God, what kind of alternative are we called to embody and offer to others?

WEEK TEN
Room for the Infinite

QUERIES AND SUGGESTIONS FOR PERSONAL REFLECTION

1. In the midst of my busyness and schedule, how am I intentionally making space and leaving room for the Infinite?

2. How do I carry a sense of sacredness into the secular world?

3. Where and when do I most experience the awesomeness of God?

4. What other queries am I being led to consider?

QUERIES AND SUGGESTIONS FOR GROUP CONVERSATION

1. Begin the gathering with a time of silence and waiting before God.

   - Focus on one person at a time. Going around the circle, have each member of the group name one way in which they see God's glory revealed in that person's life. After everyone has spoken to this person, have one of the members of the group offer a prayer of blessing for her or him.
   - Move on to the next person until the circle is completed.

2. Are there ways we can eliminate unnecessary activities from our Church/Meeting calendar, to create additional space for God and fellowship with another? What stops us from doing so?

3. What other queries are we being led to consider?

LIVING INTO THE ETERNAL PROMISE

1. As you transition from one activity to the next or from place to place, practice noticing how and where God is present. As you do, move into that space and imagine yourself in partnership with what God is doing.

2. With others around you, name the experiences of wonder, glory, goodness, or majesty you've experienced this day. Give thanks for these moments.

3. Make a choice to remove any unnecessary distraction that is crowding your life or hindering your ability to see or hear Christ.

4. What other steps am I being called to take?

WEEK ELEVEN
Secret Seekers

QUERIES AND SUGGESTIONS FOR PERSONAL REFLECTION

1. In what ways have I experienced God searching *for me?*

2. What am I still searching for in my life with God? Do I feel like something is missing?

3. If I had to describe my intentional pursuit of God in this season of life, what word would I choose? Running? Walking? Limping? Crawling? Back-peddling? Sprinting? What other word best fits and why?

4. What other queries am I being led to consider?

QUERIES AND SUGGESTIONS FOR GROUP CONVERSATION

1. Who are the "secret seekers" in our sphere of influence? In what ways are we offering an invitation for others to join us in our life together and life with God?

2. Kelly describes different ways to "run to God." Some seek God in nature. Others experience God in service. Others pursue God through the study of the Bible. While all of these are helpful, he suggests there is a Divine Center within each of us whereby we can encounter God most deeply and directly. How do each of us describe our experience of this Center? What are the paths that lead us to this place?

3. Kelly speaks often of "power." What visible signs of God's power are we seeing expressed or embodied in our community of faith?

4. What other queries are we being led to consider?

LIVING INTO THE ETERNAL PROMISE

1. Choose joy today by gratefully receiving whatever comes your way. Give thanks to God for each experience and encounter. Embrace each opportunity as a gift.

2. Choose peace today by letting go of fear and no longer fretting over what is outside your control. Seek to reconcile and be reconciled in your relationships with others. Trust the Light you are given at any moment and take the next right step in confidence.

3. Choose surrender today by letting go of your agenda and by not demanding your way. Yield to the flow of God's Spirit at work in you and through you, rather than forging your own path.

4. Choose attentiveness today by constantly turning your attention to God. At moments when you lose focus, spend no time feeling badly or wallowing in regret, simply return in glad awareness to One who is with you always.

5. What other steps am I being called to take?

WEEK TWELVE
Reflections

QUERIES AND SUGGESTIONS FOR PERSONAL REFLECTION

1. Write down glimpses of the Holy this week and reflect on them. What, if anything, do they teach you? Is there any sort of connection between them?

2. Write down your dreams each morning. Do you sense God speaking to you in any of them? If so, how?

3. Begin to write your spiritual autobiography (see below).

4. What other queries am I being led to consider?

QUERIES AND SUGGESTIONS FOR GROUP CONVERSATION

1. Have each person come prepared to share some of their spiritual autobiography with the members of the group.

2. Divide the time in equal amounts so that everyone has time to do some sharing. Better yet, consider spending several weeks on this exercise. This is often an intense and inspiring exercise that helps form a deeper spirit of community. Creating space for expansive sharing may be a great way for the group to invest in itself.

3. These practices may help you prepare you spiritual autobiography:

- **Research:** Review old journals. Talk to parents, relatives, and friends. Connect with a mentor from the past. Look back through books that were especially formative.
- **Remembering:** When do you remember first being interested in God? God sightings? "Aha" experiences? Point of conversion? "Pillar" or commitment moments? Important relationships? What activities or places helped you experience God most deeply? When did you find myself being transformed?
- **Reflection:** Reflect and examine your past in light of the Holy Spirit. Ask God to uncover pivotal moments, important events, "openings," etc., that led to your development and which could give you insight for what lies ahead.
- **Begin to Write:** Be creative. While a timeline is always a useful form to follow, don't feel limited by chronological order. Consider focusing on important themes or metaphors, tell your story as a parable, etc.

4. What other queries are we being led to consider?

LIVING INTO THE ETERNAL PROMISE

1. Commit to listen deeply to another person's story this week. Name the ways you see and hear God at work in them. Notice points of connection to your own story and experience.

2. Look for a concrete way to express your yourself and your faith in a manner that is outside your normal

experience or comfort zone. Try a new and creative outlet—art, writing, music, dance, poetry, something active and physical—that may open you to fresh movements of God's Spirit in your life.

3. If you have never considered the spiritual discipline of journaling—do so. On a daily basis, simply jot down what you notice, the questions that arise, the glimpses of God's glory and goodness that catch your eye. As is helpful, begin to fill in further details or to explore your thoughts more deeply.

4. What other steps am I being called to take?

WEEK THIRTEEN
Hasten unto God

QUERIES AND SUGGESTIONS FOR PERSONAL REFLECTION

1. What are the main themes I am noticing in *The Eternal Promise?*

2. What are the ways God is using this text to nudge me toward faithfulness and deeper communion? Am I seeing signs of change in my life?

3. What are the ways I tend toward "rugged individualism?" How does this hinder my life with God? My ability to be a vital member in community?

4. What other queries am I being led to consider?

QUERIES AND SUGGESTIONS FOR GROUP CONVERSATION

1. Are there ways we are each feeling pursued by God? How are we responding?

2. Do we believe it is possible for God to form the kind of beloved fellowship (Gemeinschaft) Kelly envisions in this chapter? If so, how?

3. How *do we* move from being members of a group to becoming a fellowship knit together in the Holy Spirit?

4. What other queries are we being led to consider?

LIVING INTO THE ETERNAL PROMISE

1. Look at your calendar for the coming year to schedule a weekend retreat. Either alone or with close spiritual companions, find a suitable place and space to be in God's Presence. Research available spiritual centers, Friends camps or conference centers, or monasteries to find out what options are available for guided retreats or to create your own time of renewal. If possible, look at longer retreat options. If you are in a small group, consider helping each other with childcare or other home responsibilities to make attendance possible for those who might have difficulty getting away.

2. Make a list of the qualities and priorities you most seek in a healthy and faithful spiritual community. How are you finding these in your current Meeting/Church? How might you help encourage some of the priorities that seem to be missing?

3. Love one another. Everyone. Everyday.

4. What other steps am I being called to take?

4

SECTION FOUR
Life in the Eternal Now

Many of the great saints have implied that the premier skill of the spiritual life is the ability to live in the present moment. As much as we may love and long for our past or eagerly look toward the future, now is the only moment in time when we can be faithful.

Life in the Eternal Now is established through a living and passionate pursuit of Christ. It is surrounded and enlivened by the fellowship of similarly hungry souls and it is fleshed out each and every day in the events and activities of our otherwise ordinary lives. Within any present moment, the ordinary has the capacity to become extra-ordinary as it is infused with the Divine Presence.

At a time in history marred by growing tensions, terrorism, heightened insecurity and alienation, the spirit of darkness can feel overwhelming and oppressive. There is a crying need for an alternative—for a band of otherwise ordinary people to be kindled by the Light of Christ and to offer the world hope and evidence that the darkness will cannot overcome it. Will we act on our call to embody and offer an alternative for others?

WEEK FOURTEEN
Have You Ever Seen a Miracle?

QUERIES AND SUGGESTIONS FOR PERSONAL REFLECTION

1. What miracles have I experienced in my life?

2. If someone were to ask me if God is merely a rumor—what would I say?

3. Thomas Kelly, like the Apostle Paul, lays important stress on our need to "die to self." Less a once-and-for-all act carried out in a distinct moment in time, the process of dying to oneself more resembles cutting off the food supply that feeds our old and broken ways. If this is true, how am I starving pride? Selfishness? Bitterness? Hatred? In the same way, how am I feeding compassion? Love? Generosity? Joy? Justice?

4. What other queries am I being led to consider?

QUERIES AND SUGGESTIONS FOR GROUP CONVERSATION

1. Share the most significant miracles we have experienced around the circle. Whether relatively large or small, how and why did these impact us the most?

2. What are the areas of selfishness we each have trouble letting go? Confess these to one another and pray for those willing to share. As a Meeting/Church, are

there expectations we may be demanding of God in order for us to feel satisfied and content in our life together? If so, confess these and pray for grace to release them.

3. How are we encouraging the ministers among us? Are there ways we can help them avoid growing weary, discouraged, or cynical in their service and leadership among us?

4. What other queries are we being led to consider?

LIVING INTO THE ETERNAL PROMISE

1. Be on the lookout for the miraculous each and every day.

2. When most tempted to exert your own way or to demand a certain outcome, be open to praying, "Father, into your hands I commit my spirit."

3. Be willing to look at your personal relationships and community connections. Am I someone who is committed to working on behalf of the marginalized and forgotten? Am I also someone building authentic and mutual friendships with members of other communities?

4. What other steps am I being called to take?

WEEK FIFTEEN
Children of the Light

QUERIES AND SUGGESTIONS FOR PERSONAL REFLECTION

1. As I look at the world in which I live and serve, am I more apt to be frightened by the darkness or captured by the Light? How can I grow in my ability to notice the Light?

2. Are there ways in which I knowingly profess what I do not yet possess in my life?

3. Am I willing to pray that God will make my life a shining light for others? If not, why not?

4. What other queries am I being led to consider?

QUERIES AND SUGGESTIONS FOR GROUP CONVERSATION

1. Going around the circle, allow each person to share specific ways the group can hold them in prayer and offer support over the next several weeks.

2. Hopefully, over the last several weeks together, we have made a start toward becoming a community of Light. Are there ways we are feeling called to continue this experiment together? What next step(s) will we take in building this fellowship?

3. Who else in our Meeting/Church might we invite to join us in this journey?

4. What other queries are we being led to consider?

LIVING INTO THE ETERNAL PROMISE

1. Be a trustworthy friend—one who walks in humility before God, with integrity before others and in harmony with what one professes.

2. Commit to flourish where you are unless clearly called away. Choose to sink your roots deeply where you have been planted. Become actively involved in your Meeting/Church. Be that kindled life that may be necessary to ignite a much more passionate and faithful fellowship. By word and deed, point others to a deeper life of communion with Christ, an increasingly beloved fellowship, and life of sacrificial service.

3. Give thanks.

4. What other steps am I being called to take?